FLY and Fall

Stefanie Golisch

Culicidae Press, LLC
918 5th Street
Ames, IA 50010
USA
www.culicidaepress.com

editor@culicidaepress.com

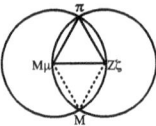

Ames | Berlin | Gainesville | Rome

FLY AND FALL
Copyright © 2014 by Stefanie Golisch. All rights reserved.

No part of this book may be reproduced in any form by any electronic or mechanized means (including photocopying, recording, or information storage and retrieval) without written permission, except in the case of brief quotations embodied in critical articles and reviews.

Respect copyrights, encourage creativity!

For more information please visit www.culicidaepress.com

ISBN-10: 1941892000
ISBN: 978-1-941892-00-8

Cover image by Francesco Balsamo. For more information go to www.francescobalsamo.it
Cover design and interior layout © 2014 by polytekton.com

Only that which does not teach, which does not cry out, which does not condescend, which does not explain, is irresistible.

W. B. Yeats

Contents

An I and His Animal   6
    Un io e la sua bestia   7
Milk and Honey   8
    Latte e miele   9
Kartoffelfeuer   10
    Kartoffelfeuer   11
Kisses   12
My Inviolability   14
    La mia inviolabilità   15
Fly and Fall   16
The Cheapest Motel Ever   18
    Il motel più economico   19
Heaven   20
Life is About All This   22
    La vita è tutto questo   23
Little Hope   24
    Little Hope   25
A Kingdom   26
Break and Be   28
First Day of the New Year   30
Mother's Body on Earth   32
    Corpo di madre sulla terra   33
Today   34
I'm the Winter   36
    Sono l'inverno   38

Alive	40
Happy Man	42
Happy Man	44
Welcoming Myshkin	46
Il mestiere di soccombere	48
When an Old Nun Gets Ready for the Night	50
Quando una vecchia suora si prepara per la notte	52
Evening Gown	54
Epitaph for a Thirteen-Year-Old Girl	56
Epitaffio per una tredicenne	58
My Knight of the Mournful Countenance	60
Mio cavaliere della Triste Figura	61
Woman, Singing for her Beloved	62
Donna che canta per il suo amato	64
Three Matches	66
Waiting for Something Like Autumn	68
La parola autunno	70
Epitaph for a Worn-Out Year	72
Del maldestro vivere	73
This Girl	74
Instead of an Afterword: Wandering Poetry	77
About the Author	81

An I and His Animal

Welcome to my heart, dear friend,
my only one, my animal.
Your hairy gray may
cover my pale skin,
delighted to become our
burning desire

Together we will be
the shameful contradiction
of the first and second world

In our saddest coldness
life burns,
truly treasured by both of us,
an I and his abiding
animal

Please do not hate me just because
I'm trying to discover who you are,
give me a hint, bite me,
so that I shall become real to
the keeper of my beastly
secret

In my warm bowels
I need to feel you belch and bark.
Do not abandon me, stay
to protect my poor I
from the hopelessness of
mankind

Un io e la sua bestia

Sotto il tuo grigio pelo
dormo vestita di pallore.
Dentro le mie calde viscere
sento il tuo ansimare secolare
mischiarsi alla mia linfa.
I tuoi morsi mi risvegliano reale,
Nel nostro unico silenzio
gorgoglia vita indistinta.
Proteggi, mia bestia,
il mio io troppo lieve
dalla mestizia degli uomini

Milk and Honey

Under the skinny April moon
she makes her home in a glass cage,
spreading her dearest things around,
half-broken beer bottles,
dead young mice.
Then she lets her body
gently slip to the ground

Neither does she want to be a bad girl,
nor a symbol or a provocation.
She is just so tired
that she can hardly keep her eyes open
any longer.
And, alas, even though tonight
she is really the filthiest thing in town,
she does look beautiful
with this blossom clenched in her fist.
An old Vietnamese woman
has carved it for her from a beet
at the end of an endless day.
Who knows what this gift was meant to be?
Maybe it was just her way to say:
good luck little girl,
on your presumably very short way to
heaven

Then she too had fallen asleep,
putting, as every night,
a violent green sheet of crepe paper
underneath her milk white head

Latte e miele

All'ora blu si fa cadere dove capita,
smistando intorno le cose più care,
bottiglie rotte di birra, topi morti,
una bambola senza occhi.
Non vuole essere una bambina cattiva,
né un simbolo, né una provocazione,
è solo stanca.
E anche se questa sera
è l'essere più lurido di tutta la città,
è bellissima con questo fiore in mano.
Una vecchia vietnamita l'ha inciso per lei
in una barbabietola alla fine
di una giornata color acqua
come per dire: buona fortuna, ragazza randagia
nel tuo probabilmente breve viaggio in cielo.
Poi, si era addormentata anche lei
posando, come tutte le notti,
un foglio di carta crespa verde violento
sotto i capelli bianchi latte

Kartoffelfeuer

The early autumn stillness holds
a sudden raven screaming,
the smell of ripe apples,
of spring rolls,
coming from the Chinese restaurant
on the first floor

There is in all this
an urge for answers to summer's ending,
that dull September afternoon,
burning my childhood
in a *Kartoffelfeuer*

The next day this smell was gone forever.
In the mirror over the lavatory,
anygirl is smiling seductively
to the new born world as if to say,
here I am,
take me
I'm yours

* A *Kartoffelfeuer* is a fire, farmers make after the harvest from the dried stalks of the potato plants.

Kartoffelfeuer

Profumo di mele mature
e di involtini primavera
dal ristorante cinese
al pian terreno

Come rispondere alla fine dell'estate,
una cupa giornata di settembre
che bruciò la mia infanzia
in un *Kartoffelfeuer*?

L'indomani sveglierà
una ragazza nuova,
sorridente al mondo appena nato.
Eccomi,
prendimi,
sono tua

---

* Il *Kartoffelfeuer* è il fuoco col quale, nelle campagne, i contadini bruciano le piante di patate successivamente al raccolto.

Kisses

Golden September, he thought,
I'll take her to the park,
treat her to a coffee,
maybe recite some verse, tell her
a funny story, true or not, who cares?
Tell her how beautiful she is
in the rosy afternoon sunlight

The truth is that for seven endless years
I haven't kissed a woman.
How can I tell her,
please let yourself be kissed
by this old man you hardly know?
Don't worry, just close your eyes
if you think that I'm too ugly,
my skin too wrinkled and
my breath too muddy.
I will not be offended and
your vanishing beauty will perfectly
understand what it is all about

Don't ask me if the stories I tell you
are true or not.
(Of course they are not, as you well know!)
Please, just let yourself be kissed
by the dry lips of a man
who senses that there isn't much time left.
Call it love or horniness or simply
fear of death,
call it whatever you like, but please,
let yourself be kissed,
since you are old enough to know
that in the world there is more than
one reason to kiss

Golden September.
Did I not choose the right season,
trying so hard to be what once was
considered romantic?
Believe me,
if I had a more exciting kiss to offer,
I would. But I have not.
This harsh tongue is all that is left of me.
I beg you, don't refuse it.
Please understand that
I'm just trying to stay alive

Alive

My Inviolability

Luz is the name of the tiniest
among my bones.
From its improbability, I'll be recreated
after the big wave
will have taken me away,
my mother will have called me
back to the sea

Dearest thing on earth,
do not forget
that my left leg is shorter
than the right one,
do not forget my folly
when evening comes,
when birds' voices die
and question after question stands still,
unanswered,
unanswerable

And I become glassy,
diaphanous,
no longer a thinking thing on earth,
much less than an I,
a waiting only

in the mystery of my imperfection

* In the Jewish religion *luz* is the name of a very tiny bone that is impossible to be destroyed and from which, at the end of time, the individual will be recreated.

La mia inviolabilità

Luz è il nome dell'osso pietra
dalla cui improbabilità, risorgerò
dopo che la grande onda
mi avrà trascinato via,
mia madre mi avrà richiamato a casa

Dormo innanzi alla parola,
metafora nascente

della mia imperfezione d'uomo

* Nella religione ebraica *luz* è il nome di un osso minuscolo,
indistruttibile e dal quale, alla fine dei tempi, l'uomo sarà ricreato.

Fly and Fall

See love, how the day slowly opens its left eye,
wide to welcome the late August morning,
see love, all this is going to happen today:

Someone will find his true love
and someone will lose it.
Someone will be arriving at the train station
just in time,
tired and pretty dirty, but not too late,
and someone will be waiting in vain.
A blackbird whispers in the ear of another,
how fresh the air is,
my friend, and how delightful it is to fly and to fall.
Someone will start the new day
with a large bottle of cheap beer while
someone else listens to the echo
of his complicated dreams. Someone
will write and re-write a letter,
knowing that it will remain unfinished,
and in someone's wounded heart not a word
is left.
A little girl will wake up safe and sound
from bad dreams,
the beloved teddy bear in her arms,
and an old woman will wake up
only to die midmorning, because the day
deserves all this.
Fighting she will slip away
before the eyes of her beloved,
right at that moment an anxious painter discovers
the one and only blue.

In *Alice's Restaurant* people are still waiting,
and so they do at the bus stop.
Today is the day, thinks the good looking young man
while he does his morning exercises,
impatient for the battle to start again.
In the cellar of an abandoned house
a red cat, almost ashamed of itself,
is teasing a young mouse with no other intention
than to entertain the tiny little
thing

What the painter, not a genius,
just a very serious researcher,
doesn't know, is that there is no one and only blue,
but only a faraway color, faraway sound,
impossible to catch among the buzzing
of all this love-making,
dying, chatting with friends, eating and drinking
and uttering one wrong word after the other,
eager to appease today's
insatiability

The Cheapest Motel Ever

This place is no good for old lovers,
so desperately devoted to the idea of love
that they would kill,
let's say, a dog,
if this was the price to pay
for a brand new first time

But, there is no dog to kill near or far,
just two pairs of worn-out shoes
under the one and only bed
for all true lovers in the world

Come, kill me, says the dog,
if there was a dog

But, alas, there is not.
There simply is not

Il motel più economico

Questa è la camera dei vecchi amanti,
così disperatamente devoti
all'idea dell'amore
che ucciderebbero,
diciamo un cane,
se questo fosse il prezzo da pagare
per una prima volta nuova di zecca.
Ma non c'è alcun cane intorno,
soltanto due paia di scarpe consunte
sotto un unico letto
per tutti gli amanti del mondo.
Venite, uccidetemi, direbbe il cane,
se ci fosse un cane,
ma, ahimè, non c'è.

Tutto qui: non c'è

Heaven

Nobody takes care of him anymore.
The color of his shabby pants is faded,
his shoes are all worn out.
Among all the beautiful girls
walking around in their sunny
Sunday afternoon,
he is a hairy gray monster,
and he knows it well

The good times, if there ever were any,
are gone.
He hardly remembers how it feels
when all of a sudden all birds fly free.
Now, everything is just a falling of
rotten apples
clumsily to the ground

Hopelessness breathes him,
and he almost would have given up
if it was not for that fat old crow,
that came sitting on his left shoulder one day.
Are you ready my friend,
will you sing with me?
What is your song about?

The beauty of decrepitude,
the very hard work to bid farewell,
life doesn't stop
bending you. Look
at all these girls in their light-green dresses,
listen to their laughter, their silly chatter,
feel their reckless desire for love
on your hunch,
tremble with them once again
and caw with me

Caw

Life is About All This

You are marvelous. The gods wait to delight in you.
                                                    Charles Bukowski

Hunting wild animals and cooking them
on an open fire.
Sad flowers at the end of a late Summer's day
(will they ever awake to new life?)
Craws, spelling the senselessness
of grieving to the blind sky.
The copy of the copy of the holy drinker,
you can find his kind in every little town
in the world.
The old lady who first lost her elder brother,
then her elder sister, knowing that now it's her turn.
The most ordinary girl in town,
in her cheap jeans, her cheap T-shirt,
and her unimaginable dreams.
The new old couple at their first kiss,
scared and eager
to be revived in the dreams of the other.
November sun, purple time,
time to be reborn, time to say sorry,
and time to forgive. The year ending
is a worn-out pair of shoes
after an endless walk in a baroque labyrinth.
A verse written by Hölderlin, saying
that the happier a man is,
the easier he ruins himself.
The mystery of every new day
and the seven hidden meanings of an old
fairy tale.
Dark German woods and fair Italian beauty.
The idea that a rotten sock can be mended,
that bleeding wounds can heal,
and that our singing can improve
by and by, if only we let our voice merge

with all voices

La vita è tutto questo

You are marvellous. The gods wait to delight in you.
Charles Bukowski

Stanchi di essere una promessa.

L'uomo corvo in partenza per il reale.
Ragazza finta bionda, finta allegra, finta viva.
Gobbo, appoggiato su un bastone di seta.
La coppia di nani al loro primo bacio,
ansiosi di piacere ai grandi.
Sole di Novembre, vuoto di metafore.
Un verso di Hölderlin che recita:
più l'uomo è felice,
più alto è il rischio che si rovini.
Il mistero di ogni nuovo giorno
e i sette significati nascosti
di una antica fiaba.
La fiducia che una calza rotta
possa essere rammendata,
che le ferite possano guarire,
e che la nostra voce possa migliorare
con il tempo,
confondendosi

con tutte le voci

Little Hope

She sells herself at the fish market.
Her prices are good and she smiles
at everybody who comes along,
stinking of fish, drunk at sunrise.
Little Hope never says no and never stops
smiling.
If she had the words, she might say,
what do you want, desire is the only reality,
but, of course, she has not,
girl in her shortest tiger skirt.
In her bowels, every man is welcome
just the way he deserves.
When she's sold out, around noon or so,
her body is a kingdom lost and found.
Like a child she falls asleep,
a snow flake in the middle of an August day,
pure like the eyes of a dead
flatfish

Little Hope

Si offre al mercato del pesce.
I suoi prezzi sono buoni. Sorride
a tutti quelli che passano,
puzzolenti, ubriachi all'alba.
Little Hope non dice mai di no
e non smette mai di sorridere.
Se avesse le parole, direbbe,
cosa vuoi, il desiderio è l'unica realtà.
Nelle sue viscere ogni uomo è benvenuto
nel modo in cui lo desidera.
Quando verso mezzogiorno è esaurita,
il suo corpo è un reame
perduto e ritrovato.
Come una bambina cade nel sonno,
fiocco di neve in una giornata d'agosto,
pura come l'occhio morto
del pesce luna

A Kingdom

Look what is left for you in my battered hands:
a shard of green glass, softened around
the edges
a withered chestnut
a poor deaf feather
a tortoiseshell
a piece of a broken heart

I'm a waste

Please take these precious things
and merge them with your own
leaves and buttons and laces,
then sink with them
deeper and deeper
into the dreams of the
unlikely unicorn

Believe me, love,
there is no other kingdom to conquer.
There simply is not

Amo le tue cose inutili.
Impara tu ad amare le mie.

Break and Be

Very last day of the worn-out year

A pair of dusty red ballerina pumps
in an old suitcase in the cellar.
Once they were brand new,
waiting impatiently in the little shoe shop
downtown,
the most desirable thing in the world.

The girl I once was
would have given everything
to possess them,
to make them dance into New Year's heart,
to make them dance
forever

Will they ever dance again?
Or are they possibly still dancing
on the unwashed feet of a chubby girl
whose name I will never know?

Wear them for me tonight, anygirl,
make them dance,
make them as happy as you can,
that's to say, unaware of their happiness

Make them break.
Break and be.

Just be

First Day of the New Year

What does a bird know about such things as heaviness and lightness?

Without me you are not

Without my effort
to guess your colors,
nameless you must remain,
your word unspoken,
your work undone

I need you
and you need him,
little Chinese boy
cutting trees and dragonflies silently
out of beets
in a crowded *vicolo*
in the old town of Rome

How easy it is to overlook
those who don't care to be seen,
to forget them that very moment
your eyes meet

But you do not,
eager as you are
for lightness and heaviness,
antique amphora
waiting to be filled with water and
wine,
fish reaching the shore,
turning into birds and bears and homo sapiens,
calling things and each other by names,
trying very hard to be landmarks
for gods with animal masks

"Wenn Gott Mensch werden konnte, kann er auch Katze werden," sagte die Portugiesin, und er hätte ihr die Hand vor den Mund halten müssen, wegen der Gotteslästerung, aber sie wußten, kein Laut davon drang aus diesen Mauern hinaus."

Robert Musil: *Die Portugiesin*

Mother's Body on Earth

When will we three meet again?
In thunder, lightning or in rain
When the hurlyburly's done,
When the battle's lost and won.

Shakespeare, *Macbeth*

Lying in the street
with nothing on but her pale skin,
eyes wide open,
my mother's body on earth
is a wound

On its very short way to last coldness
her ungiving flesh
deeply deserves mine,
warm and still bleeding,
to cover her shame

Here we are, mother,
the battle is over.
Dead horses and warriors
welcoming us in a legendary land
where winners and losers
will never stop fighting
for forgiveness

Corpo di madre sulla terra

When will we three meet again?
In thunder, lightning or in rain?
When the hurlyburly's done,
When the battle's lost and won.

Shakespeare, *Macbeth*

Stesa sull'asfalto
il corpo di mia madre
è una ferita

Sulla breve via verso il freddo,
la mia carne copre
la nostra sconfitta
a malapena

La battaglia è finita.
Nelle bocche spalancate
dei guerrieri morenti
ti canto, madre,
una ninnananna alla rovescia

Today

As helpless as an old goldfish in its eternal crystal cage

Three desires, three choices rather,
that's what it is all about

Either you let your dreams die,
you sell them at the market
or you believe in them,
in spite of everything

In spite of everything,
she's bent on being the belief
that once upon a time
when the world comes to the world again,
little fish
will fly lightweight to the mud
where the fire salamander hides

the secret of inviolacy

I'm the Winter

for G.K.

The play has four main parts,
Spring, Summer, Autumn and Winter.
Of course, the prettiest little girl
in her pink dress, will be lovely as Spring.
Another one, dark haired, the opposite kind of
beauty,
is the melancholic image of a late
Summer's day.
A big boy with heavy bones
lowers himself to embody an autumnal
tempest.
There is something exciting
about the idea of destroying
the peerless beauty of the two girls.
Now, only Winter is left.
Come on, says the teacher,
looking around searchingly,
who wants to be Winter?
I'm the Winter, he says, standing up.
And since nobody else is asking for this part,
he gets it immediately.
Shrouded in a floral white sheet,
with white gloves and a white cotton beard,
covering almost his entire face,
the lanky boy with his deep-set gray eyes is, indeed,
the ideal incarnation of wintertime.
His clumsy dance is a gentle snowfall
in the middle of a moonlit night,
and, all of a sudden, a wild snow storm

At the end of January,
his companions, armed with sticks and pitchforks,
enter the scene,
yelling and screaming to chase Winter away,
but he, contrary to what he was told to,
doesn't move,
looking straight into the audience
of sheepishly smiling parents and teachers,
as if looking for help,
but help doesn't come and never will

At the end of the evening, in a corner of the gym,
we can see Winter carefully taking off his beard,
looking at it for a long time

Sono l'inverno

a G.K.

Quattro sono i ruoli principali,
primavera, estate, autunno, inverno.
La bambina più carina con il suo vestito rosa
sarà amabile come la primavera.
Un'altra, con i capelli scuri, il tipo di bellezza
opposto,
è l'immagine melanconica della tarda
estate.
Un bambino robusto dalle ossa pesanti
incarnerà un temporale d'autunno.
Ora manca solo l'inverno.
Sù, dice la maestra, chi è l'inverno?
Io sono l'inverno, dice lui e si alza
in piedi.
Avvolto in un lenzuolo bianco
con dei guanti bianchi e una bianca
barba di cotone che quasi gli nasconde il viso,
quel bambino dai piccoli occhi grigioverdi *è*
l'inverno
che ora nevica, ora tace, ora tempesta.
Alla fine di gennaio entrano in scena
i suoi compagni,
armati di bastoni e forconi per cacciarlo via.
Ma lui non si muove,
guardando dritto nei sorrisi stolti di madri e maestre
come per chiedere aiuto,
ma nessun aiuto viene

Più tardi, in un angolo della palestra,
ecco l'inverno che lento si toglie la barba
fissando il suo nudo volto a lungo
in una scheggia
di specchio

Alive

This is the very last hour of an old life,
school is a worn-out pair of shoes,
too small, too shabby,
it simply doesn't fit any more

Laughter and bawling, bustling about,
throwing things out of the window,
kicking little paper balls at the wall,
munching potato chips, hustling one another

Inside and outside:
a hot tiger cage, placed in the middle
of an early Summer's day,
the gentle smell of lime blossoms
filling the air with promises

This is the very last hour of an old life
stories about teachers are told,
stupid little anecdotes about a fat blond
spinster,
a never-smiling nun,
poor things who live and die
and are buried right now, right here,
in this classroom coffin

They are the past.
At the age of nineteen,
the past is an old pigeon,
dying silently at the roadside.
There is something much better,
called future.
And something even better,
called today

And they have it.
Here they are,
waiting impatiently for the school bell
to ring for the very last time,
here they are, tremendously alive

in their perfect bodies of liquid light

Happy Man

In his off-white linen suit and his panama,
he seems to step right out of a Chekhov play
where people talk and talk
and nothing ever happens

He is all nineteenth century,
except for his yellow racing bike.
At the age of eighty-four,
he is full of expectations.
In spite of everything,
life is a magnificent magnolia blossom,
slowly opening its newborn petals like a
woman
undressing in front of her beloved
for the first time

Unfortunately or not, he says smilingly,
I haven't met
the great love of my life yet,
in other words, there is a woman,
somewhere in the world,
waiting to be found and finally
kissed awake
by the old man I have become
over the very hard work of
living

In the cherry orchard
the afternoon fills up delicately
with all the battles
which we proudly consider unique

(In his speech on Pushkin,
Dostoevsky defines a Russian
as a man who understands all men.)

The last thing I see of him
is how he gets on his bike,
a little insecure,
but also careless about his insecurity,
riding away into a splendid evening
of unfulfilled promises,
as happy as a man on earth can
be

Happy Man

Nel suo abito estivo color panna e il panama,
sembra appena uscito da una commedia
di Čechov
dove si parla senza tregua,
e nulla mai succede.
Lui è tutto diciannovesimo secolo,
tranne che per la bicicletta da corsa gialla.
All'età di ottantaquattro anni,
vibra di aspettative.
La vita è una magnolia
che lenta apre i petali come una donna
che si spoglia davanti al suo amato
per la prima volta.
Non ho ancora, dice sorridendo,
incontrato l'amore della mia vita.
Da qualche parte quindi
attende una donna
di essere destata con un bacio
da questo vecchio che il mestiere di vivere
ha forgiato a fatica.
Nel giardino dei ciliegi,
il pomeriggio lievemente si riempie
di battaglie e banalità.
L'ultima immagine di lui è come monta
in bicicletta,
un poco insicuro, ma senza troppo
curarsene,
pedalando in una sera di promesse,
felice come un uomo sulla terra
può essere

Welcoming Myshkin

How easy it is to love him,
to be totally on his side,
as long as he doesn't step out of the pages
of the *Idiot*,
as long as he doesn't smell badly,
laugh sharply without any reason,
saying things a brave man cannot
confess.
He is the one birds have chosen for company,
the one who senses
hardship and happiness by the sound
of their early morning singing

Every once in a while he appears
in the middle of life,
a strange hat with a pheasant feather
on his head.
There he is, standing next to you like
an old friend,
and in fact, you have known him for quite a long
time.
He was your classmate in elementary school,
the pale, fat kid, the others were mocking
from the first day on.
Some years later he was an awkward boy,
shyly in love with you.

You were fourteen, and the only reason
you let yourself be kissed
was a half-assed feeling of pity for him.
Then you took to your heels,
deeply ashamed of your cowardly kindness.
He is the always friendly smiling man
at the bus stop,
the inconspicuous colleague
with the water-blue eyes,
nobody is willing to waste
his coffee break on,
easy to overlook, easy to despise,
easy to forget
in a flash

He is the one birds have chosen
for company,
the one to defend the unbroken
defenselessness on earth,
the hardest art to succumb

Il mestiere di soccombere

Ci perdoni la nostra felicità.
　　　　　　　　Dostoevskij, L'idiota

Stare dalla sua parte non è difficile
finché non esce dalle pagine dell'*Idiota*,
finché non si deve sopportare la puzza
di sudore e i suoi piccoli singhiozzi
acuti

Alle elementari era il tuo compagno
di banco,
un bambino roseo,
preso di mira fin dal primo giorno.
Qualche anno dopo
era il ragazzo impacciato,
timidamente innamorato di te,
un breve bacio di pietà e
un lungo imbarazzo
di fronte alla tua debole
gentilezza.
E' l'uomo di vetro alla fermata del tram,
il collega degli gli occhi blu acqua,
con il quale nessuno vuole sprecare
l'intervallo, la ragazza degli scorpioni
che ricama un corredo di vento e terra
per la sposa di
nessuno,
maestra del mestiere più difficile
di soccombere

When an Old Nun Gets Ready for the Night

When an old nun gets ready for the night,
the first thing she will take off
are her heavy brown boots,
then she'll get rid of her veil,
closed in the back with a Velcro strip,
and finally she will open the long zipper
in the back of her habit and
let it fall to the ground

In her yellowed underskirt she is standing
in the middle of her mirrorless cell.
Instead of her own image,
Jesus, a young man with long blond curls
is smiling at her seductively as if wanting to say,
don't be shy, go ahead,
are you or are you not my beloved
bride?

And of course she is.

Trusting she takes off her skin-colored stockings,
her skin-colored bra and
her skin-colored underpants.
In the merciful half light of a cold autumn night,
there she is,
mother-naked before her master.

Then she quickly gets into her pink nightgown
with little white daisies.
Shivering she slips under the waveless,
snow-white sheets
that have been waiting for her all day
long.
Lost like a raindrop in a cloudless sky
she lets her weary fingers
disappear in the holy space between her legs
where life hides away

humid, dark, mute

Quando una vecchia suora si prepara per la notte

Quando una vecchia suora si prepara per la notte,
in principio si toglie
le pesanti scarpe marroni,
poi il velo, chiuso dietro la nuca
con una striscia di velcro.
Aprendo la lunga cerniera sulla schiena,
lascia cadere la tonaca
a terra.
Nella sua veste ingiallita sta davanti
a nessuno specchio.
Invece della propria immagine,
le sorride seducente
un giovane uomo dai lunghi riccioli biondi
che dice:
non aver paura, sei o non sei la mia sposa
diletta?
Fiduciosa, sfila i collant color pelle,
il reggiseno color pelle e le mutande color pelle.
Nella luce diffusa di una fredda notte d'autunno,
eccola, completamente nuda
davanti al suo Signore.
Tremando, indossa una camicia da notte
rosa,
e si fa scivolare sotto le coperte.
Persa come una goccia di pioggia
in un cielo senza nuvole,
fa sparire le dita stanche nell'antro sacro
tra le gambe,
dove si nasconde la vita

umida, buia, muta

Evening Gown

Handmade.
She loves nice fabrics, blinking buttons,
shiny silk ribbons.
Making life somehow more colorful, you know,
she says.
When she came to the United States from
Puerto Rico
in the early sixties, she was not even seventeen,
working in textile factories in the Paterson area
for a dollar an hour, sleeping in one bed
with both her sisters.
That was not a good life, she says,
but the Lord made it become a better one.
He called me and this was my answer.
Nuns have a good life, they must not worry about
anything,
food and stuff like that.
In her free time she dreams up robes,
fanciful outfits for glamorous events.
A night-blue one with red and purple stars
is her lastest creation

Did you try it on, sister Rufina,
did you take a look at yourself in the mirror?
Take it, she says, tell your daughter to make it
dance.
Then she puts on her apron
—little red roses on a light yellow ground—
and turns

away

Epitaph for a Thirteen-Year-Old Girl

It was by chance that I discovered her grave.

I was looking for nothing that day,
just taking a walk through the cemetery of my hometown,
reading the still familiar surnames,
a whole world enclosed in their sedate sound.
November 1974. She was not sick that day,
she didn't have a seasonal influenza,
but she was
dead.
We would not see her again.
The day before she had been run over
by a truck while riding her bike.
That was the only thing the math teacher
was able to tell us about her
death,
and about death at all.
Then he had tried very hard to get back to normal.
Some of the girls were crying,
others were laughing hysterically
or just pretending nothing had happened.
My own question was, how to behave now?
How to walk and to speak and to breathe
after death had opened the door?

We had not really been friends,
but something had grown between us
after she had confessed to me,
that a boy had kissed her.
That was, of course, the most exciting
thing in the world

Standing in front of her shabby grave,
the only consolation I can think of,
is this kiss,
given such a long time ago
that it has no importance any more
whether it was true or just a dreamt-up
little lie

Epitaffio per una tredicenne

L'avevo quasi dimenticata.
Non cercavo nulla quel giorno,
mentre passeggiavo in quel vecchio
cimitero,
fermandomi di tanto in tanto
davanti a una tomba
per leggere i cognomi familiari,
un mondo serrato in suoni remoti.
Novembre millenovecentosettantaquattro.
Non era ammalata,
non aveva l'influenza,
ma era stata travolta da un camion.
Questo fu l'unico particolare
che l'insegnante sapeva dirci sulla sua
morte
e sulla morte in generale.
Poi era passato alla
matematica.
Alcune ragazze piangevano,
altre facevano finta di niente e
io non sapevo da che parte schierarmi.
Non eravamo state amiche,
ma un giorno mi aveva raccontato
di aver baciato un ragazzo
e io ero stata indecisa se crederle o no

Davanti alla sua tomba abbandonata,
penso a quel bacio,
successo così tanto tempo fa
che non ha più alcuna importanza
se forse mi aveva
mentito

My Knight of the Mournful Countenance

That autumn he had started calling her again.
Always at the *Blue Hour*. He felt lonely,
he said, old, he said, death
was shadowing him. Who knew,
when and where and how
they would meet for the final duel?
Of course, she didn't and while
he was talking nineteen to the dozen,
she was thinking of the *Seventh seal*.
But the old man who once had been her lover
was not as brave and severe
as Antonius Block. He wasn't ready at all
for the crucial game and the purpose
of his annoying phone calls
was just to convince her to make love
to him. Listen, he said, you don't love me
any more, that's ok,
but do you not even have pity on me? Come on,
be a good girl. Sometimes she was
and sometimes she was not.
It depended on the colors of the sky,
on how the trees outside her window
were looking at her
and on how deep her own sadness had grown over
the day

Mio cavaliere della Triste Figura

In autunno aveva cominciato a chiamarla
di nuovo, sempre nel tardo pomeriggio.
Si sentiva solo, diceva, vecchio,
l'idea della morte lo perseguitava.
Chi sa quando e dove e come
si sarebbero scontrati nel duello finale.
E mentre la riempiva di chiacchiere,
lei pensava al *Settimo sigillo*.
Ma quel vecchio, un tempo suo amante,
non era coraggioso e austero come
Antonius Block.
Non era affatto pronto per la partita decisiva,
e l'unico scopo delle sue chiamate noiose
era di persuaderla a fare l'amore con
lui.
Ascolta, diceva, tu non mi ami più,
ma almeno abbi pietà di me. Sii buona.
Qualche volta lo era e qualche volta no.
Dipendeva dai colori del cielo,
dagli sguardi incorruttibili degli alberi
fuori dalla finestra
e di quanto era cresciuta
la tristezza dentro
durante le stagioni del giorno

Woman, Singing for Her Beloved

I hear her raucous voice from the street.
She cannot sing,
she doesn't know music,
she doesn't know words either and
it is already after midnight
and she is still singing and
nobody listens to her but me
who cannot stand this woman
anymore
and would rather kill her singing
for nobody and
I start throwing things at her
through the window, your beloved is
dead,
I cry, but she doesn't stop and
I try to get to sleep, but sleep
won't come and
now I get really upset and
at daybreak I throw the cat at her,
shut up, I cry, look what your stupid singing
did,

you killed the cat, but still she won't stop and
at her feet the cat is dying miserably
of its inner wounds,
this woman has no pity,
this woman cannot sing,
this woman has forgotten the cat's name,
it was *Beautiful Barry*. He was only
a few months old
when we adopted him from the animal shelter
some spring ago
or so

Donna che canta per il suo amato

Dalla strada giunge un canto
di bellezza alla rovescia.
E' già mezzanotte e non smette,
canto di donna
amato morto.
All'alba l'amato prende il gatto,
lo lancia addosso alla cantatrice
calva di cuore,
ai piedi suoi muore di pena
l'amore, il gatto,
nati qualche primavera fa

Three Matches

Don't be afraid,
when the cold comes,
I'll light the fire.
Three matches are left, as if
I had foreseen your defenselessness
when it was still sleeping
under the plumage of your
brilliancy

In those days you made
everybody
fall in love with you. You
sang your song very well, your
dance pleased the world and you
were pleased with its
pleasure.
Then, little by little, the light
stepped out of your life
into someone else's

Try not to summarize,
Try not to get things clear.
Speak low.
Just say something familiar
like, who knows weather it's going to rain
tomorrow.
And I might answer,
while looking out of the window,
time to feed the cat,
don't worry, love, I'll be right
back

Waiting for Something Like Autumn

The first time I saw him in front of the
railway station,
gray-haired, with a long nose and an
old brown suitcase,
a black umbrella tucked under his arm.
He was talking to himself about the
colors of the rain.
I had just missed the train and was undecided
whether to wait for the next one
or walk back home.
Actually, I was not waiting for any train,
but for Autumn to come, finally.
Of course, I forgot the stranger at once

The next day, I saw him downtown,
sitting on a bridge in the milky sunlight
of a late afternoon,
lost in thought, smiling gently into the sky.
For a second it seemed as if he had
recognized me,
but I might have been mistaken.
Anyway, I had no time to think about him,
busy as I was with my daily errands.
And still waiting for Autumn to come

Late one night, I saw him rummaging
through a garbage can.
I was tempted to offer him money,
but then I said to myself
that he was not asking for
anything.

And I preferred to imagine him
hungry and cold,
rather than offended by the
misery of my charity

When I saw him the following day,
our eyes met and all of a sudden I realized
that it was not by chance
that he had chosen our little town.
No doubt, he had promises to keep,
and he knew
how desperately I was waiting for Autumn
that year.
Thereafter, I saw him no longer

Dear stranger, if you were a message,
be sure that I got it:
we will never be able to tell the color of another
but there is nothing to worry about.
Or, if you prefer, let's put it this way,
wherever you may go,
someone will always be waiting
at the railway station,
undecided whether to leave or to stay,
ready to welcome the odd and the
heartbroken
as if saying hello to himself

La parola autunno

La prima volta, lo vidi davanti alla stazione,
capelli grigi, valigia scalcinata,
ombrello rosa pallido sotto il braccio.
Stava contando i colori della pioggia.
Avevo appena perso il treno
o, a dire il vero, non avevo atteso alcun
treno,
ma la parola autunno

Il giorno dopo era seduto sul Ponte dei Leoni,
disegnando con la punta dell'ombrello
dei cerchi nell'aria.
Ma non avevo tempo da perdere

Una sera lo vidi frugare nella
spazzatura.
Avrei potuto buttargli degli spiccioli,
ma non volevo offenderlo
con la miseria della mia carità

Quando lo vidi per l'ultima volta,
mi stava aspettando davanti alla
stazione.
Finalmente mi sedetti accanto a lui
per salutare insieme
quelli che sarebbero arrivati,
quelli che sarebbero partiti e quelli
che erano indecisi
sulla soglia
come se dessimo il benvenuto
a noi stessi

Epitaph for a Worn-Out Year

When help comes from Zion, we shall be like dreamers.
                                                    Psalm

When I woke up into the new day
they were still there,
hanging around on sofas and armchairs
like people in a Chekhov play,
talking and drinking and accusing
each other all the time for their infelicity.
Jesus, I thought, didn't I sent this mob
to hell last night,
didn't I tell them once for all
that I do not wish to see them anymore?
I was really upset but then an old man
in a ridiculous grass-green suit
stood up and said:
Strange enough, while I was dreaming
I knew I was dreaming
and so I told my dreams where to take me,
but they were just laughing at me
and so I got very angry
and spent the rest of the night looking
out of the window. Snow fell and fell
into my bleeding eyes and at daybreak
a feeling came over me
as if I finally understood the secret of this
whiteness

Thank you, I heard myself say to nobody,
for protecting
my dreams against the littleness of my
wishes

   * This psalm was invented by the German writer Karl Philipp
   Moritz (1765-1793).

Del maldestro vivere

Quando arriva l'aiuto da Sion, noi saremo come dei sognatori.
                                                            Salmo

Quando mi svegliai, erano ancora tutti lì,
oziosi protagonisti di una commedia di Čechov,
dove il chiacchiericcio e gli insulti non smettono
mai.
Stavo per buttarli fuori tutti quanti
quando all'improvviso un vecchio si alzò
in piedi. Strano, disse, nel sogno cercavo
di ingiungere i miei sogni,
ma quelli si prendevano beffa di me.
Per il resto della notte mi feci cadere la neve
negli occhi sanguinanti
finché all'alba la mia bocca avrebbe
pronunciato da sola
la metafora del suo cadere.
Poco pesano i nostri desideri
davanti alla legge della rinuncia, disse,
mentre dai lunghi capelli suoi nevicava
soavemente
sull' incessante brusio del nostro maldestro
vivere

* Si tratta di un salmo inventato dallo scrittore tedesco Karl Philipp Moritz (1756-1793)

This Girl

The one writing to her parents about
prices and waist, *they only use
butter, even for cooking. Benjamin
is so petted, he gets everything he wants,
sometimes
he plays dead in the bathtub, just to mock me.*
This is Paris and she is an au pair,
hired by Agnès, *femme fatale* in her early forties,
to look after the boy and to do the daily housekeeping.
*They put the cigarettes out on their plates,
what a mess,* she writes,
annoyed, because Paris was definitely meant to be
something greater.
The letter is buried in her mother's room
among papers and things
they have to get rid of as soon as possible.
Last night I went to the movies,
she reads, sitting at her mother's desk,
*it cost me ten marks,
but it was worse, because I didn't understand
a damn.*
Nothing farther away on this cold December day
than fall of 1980,
a girl, eating chocolate cookies while watching cartoons
with an eleven-year-old boy.
Things one can tell and things one cannot tell.

For a second she sees herself standing
in front of a big mirror,
trying on one of her landladies' black negligees,
bemused, as if she was the misty answer to a question
she could not ask.
While I was washing the dishes,
Agnès' new lover came into the kitchen
and put his dirty glass right into the water,
she writes, *I wanted to kill him, but of course*
I didn't.
Then she must stop,
because tonight she is going to meet
with her new friends.
If there had been other letters,
her mother must have thrown them away and
at the end of an exhausting day,
she too throws away almost everything,
except for that chubby girl in her large,
clay-colored sweater.
When she closes her eyes,
she can see her flying down *Boulevard S. Michel*
in the same rhythm the heart of Paris
beats,
revealing and concealing
at every corner of the street

what is still impossible to ask

Instead of an Afterword: Wandering Poetry

Poetry has two legs, two arms, a belly and a face,
a unique look to make things and men appear deeper,
and sometimes to turn away without a word.
Poetry is unpredictable.
Its moods might annoy the poet, but, alas, he has no choice.
Follow me, says poetry, like a seductive siren,
do not rely on me, but be my companion for the lifetime of a poem.
Poetry chooses time, place and language.
Poetry likes to arise, to hide and to disguise,
revealing and concealing itself according to a mazy law.
Poetry deserves changes, anxious to arrive at Ithaca,
but also curious to pick up what has been jettisoned on the long way there.
Ithaca is the heartbeat, the form is the open sea of poets' blood and lymph.

Fly and Fall.
Poetry invited me to enter the body of a new language,
to arrange my world in new colours, tastes, sounds.
Mother Language is big-hearted. My verses,
a small regiment of hunchbacks, were generously welcomed
and transformed.

"We have to find true words", says the Austrian poet Ingeborg Bachmann.
It may happen, that a poet knows his own language too well
to find the simplicity of truth.

The travelling eye and soul,
concentrating present, past and future in the very moment: poetry *happens*.
Look at yourself, dressed in another language.
Every language has its own metabolism.
The new, the never known word: the magic word.
Call it! Catch it! Make it become real again.
Every language has its own true words and its own lies.
Some of them are welcomed among the new signs and symbols,
some must wait before the door.
Every poem is a body, a man, a world,
waiting to entwine with reality.

You can deeply understand a poem in a language you don't know.
Its hidden truth can be blacker than black.
You, reader, will be the light.
Poetry is communication beyond facts.
Poetry tells light and shadow, greatness and misery.
'Give your words a meaning,
but give them also a shadow,' says the poet Paul Celan.
Don't sell it.
Set yourself free, but don't get lost in the arms of the one you love.

Fly and Fall.
Some poems found their way into Italian, some did not.
There are open spaces, never empty ones.
Poetry is patient.
Poetry can fall in love, poetry can be unjust,
poetry can get sick and die and resurrect.
Poetry needs eyes and ears, hearts and souls.
Poetry wants to tell and to travel,
eager to find the reader
for whom it was written for.
Poetry needs to be needed,
to be filled with water and wine, love and hate,
never with indifference.
Poetry says: touch me.
Poetry loves to look at itself in many masquerades.
Poetry says: Come closer. I contain multitudes.

Poetry wants to dance: in the light, in the dark and in the half-light of our daily work of living and loving.

About the Author

Stefanie Golisch lives, reads, and writes in Italy since 1988. Her most recent publication *Ferite: Storie di Berlino* was published by Edizioni Ensemble, Roma, in 2014.

www.ingramcontent.com/pod-product-compliance
Lightning Source LLC
Chambersburg PA
CBHW081357040426
42451CB00018B/3490